SUNLIGHT
· IN THE ·
SHADOWS

SUNLIGHT
·IN THE·
SHADOWS

The Landscape of Emily Carr

◆

Photography by
Michael Breuer

Text by
Kerry Mason Dodd

Kerry Mason Dodd

Michael Breuer

Toronto
Oxford University Press
1984

SOURCE MATERIAL

In *Sunlight in the Shadows* I have used unpublished writings by Emily Carr housed in three separate institutions:

All letters from Emily Carr to Edythe Hembroff-Schleicher are from the Provincial Archives of British Columbia in Victoria.

All letters from Emily Carr to Nan Cheney are from the University of British Columbia, Special Collections, Vancouver.

All journals, notebooks and miscellaneous notes, as well as letters from Emily Carr to Ira Dilworth, are excerpts from the Carr papers in the Public Archives of Canada in Ottawa.   KERRY MASON DODD

PHOTOGRAPHIC NOTE

All images for this book were taken with LEICA cameras and LEITZ lenses having focal lengths from 21mm to 400mm.   MICHAEL BREUER

Produced by Roger Boulton Publishing Services
Designed by Fortunato Aglialoro

© Oxford University Press (Canadian Branch) 1984
OXFORD is a trademark of Oxford University Press

1 2 3 4 — 7 6 5 4

Printed in Hong Kong by Scanner Art Services, Inc., Toronto

CANADIAN CATALOGUING IN PUBLICATION DATA

Carr, Emily, 1871–1945
   Sunlight in the shadows : the landscape of Emily Carr

Text consists of excerpts from the artist's unpublished correspondence, manuscripts and journals. Cf. Pref.
ISBN 0-19-540464-5

1. Carr, Emily, 1871–1945.   2. Painters—Canada—Biography.   I. Dodd, Kerry Mason.   II. Breuer, Michael.   III.Title.

ND249.C3A2 1984   759.11   C84-098759-5

The portrait of Emily Carr, *circa* 1900, shown on the jacket, is a detail from Photo. No. 27429 of the Provincial Archives of British Columbia and is used with their kind permission.

Preface

This book is intended to serve as a response to two great demands that arise concerning Emily Carr; one with respect to her writing and the other to her painting. The following pages will, I hope, contribute to the study and enjoyment of this eminent Canadian artist by presenting more of her fine writing and, through modern photographs, the landscape of British Columbia which inspired her.

Here is fresh material for the avid admirer who is always hungry for more of her writing. I am delighted to be able to present 'new' writings which in Carr's own inimitable style describe and ponder the landscape and her experiences on sketching trips to various parts of British Columbia. I sought in her unpublished correspondence, manuscripts and journals, those thoughts, observations and descriptions which best reveal the strength of her bond with British Columbia. I have respected Emily Carr's wish that the editor would 'punctuate and let me be.' Some of these excerpts from Carr's personal writings were selected for the power of their imagery; others for their sensitivity or wit. In every instance her clear, original and energetic thoughts complement and expand the photographic image.

Michael Breuer's superb photographs of British Columbia answer the other demand, which relates primarily to Carr's painting. People from all parts of the world have said to me, 'Now that I've come to British Columbia I understand her paintings so much better.' When given the opportunity by Oxford University Press to produce a book showing the 'beloved West' of Emily Carr I accepted the challenge with enthusiasm. This was an aspect of her work which had not yet been presented, yet the landscape so near and dear to Emily Carr is as dynamic and unique as she was herself. A walk in our rain forest, for example, can't help but bring Emily Carr's painting to mind. This landscape evokes the astonishing feeling of stepping into *Sombreness Sunlit* or *Forest Landscape II* or any one of a number of her paintings. It was a formidable task for Michael Breuer, equipped with a long list of place names in British Columbia, to capture Emily Carr's world with his camera. Having found a spot which had been a sketching site of Emily's he had to determine what it was about that particular spot which would have interested her.

We have many people to thank for helping to make this book possible. Permission to publish Emily Carr's correspondence, journals, and miscellaneous writings was most kindly and generously given to me by Mr Jack Parnall. I am also grateful to Dr Wilfred Smith, Dominion Archivist, and Mr John Bovey, Provincial Archivist of British Columbia, for giving me access to the Carr holdings in their respective archives. Thanks also go to Frances Gundry, Head of Manuscripts and Government Records, Provincial Archives of British Columbia, and to George Brandak of Special Collections at the University of British Columbia.

We appreciate the generosity of Mrs Margaret Hutton-Potts (now Mme Chantreau) who, as owner of the 'House of All Sorts', allowed us to view and photograph Emily Carr's attic ceiling. Marjorie and Barbara Richardson, Dawn Fitzpatrick and many others (forgive us for not listing you all) deserve our sincerest thanks for the parts they played in the creation of this volume.

I am especially indebted to Mrs Edythe Hembroff-Schleicher for her support and encouragement.

I dedicate all of my work for this book to my daughter, Sarah, who has patiently shared her mother with Emily Carr.

KERRY MASON DODD

Introduction

Emily Carr was born on 13 December 1871 in Victoria, British Columbia. Of British descent, she was the second youngest of nine children born to Emily (née Saunders) and Richard Carr. Destined to become one of Canada's most distinctive painters, Emily Carr showed promise as an artist at an early age. Her father encouraged his youngest daughter in artistic endeavours, providing her with drawing and painting classes, which Emily much preferred to regular schooling.

In 1891, shortly after her parents' deaths, Emily resolved to strike out on her own and become an artist. She extracted permission from her legal guardian to attend the California School of Design in San Francisco, at that time the closest serious art school. Two and a half years later, Emily Carr returned to Victoria determined to continue as an artist and converted the loft of the barn on the family property to a studio where she successfully taught art classes to children. Having already conceived the idea of going to Paris or London in order to advance her studies in painting, she began to save in anticipation of her journey, hoarding hard-earned money in a pair of old boots hung in the loft of her barn studio.

During the summer of 1898 Emily, then in her twenty-seventh year, made the first of many important trips to Indian villages throughout British Columbia. She travelled by steamer up the west coast of Vancouver Island to the Indian village of Ucluelet and there the seed germinated of what was to become a lifelong interest in the Indian people and culture. Much of Emily Carr's early work centres on the Indian villages and people; attesting to her affinity for the Indian culture is her tremendous output of totem pole sketches and paintings, particularly between 1907 and 1913.

With the proceeds of her art classes Emily Carr was able by 1899 to finance a trip to London to further her studies at the Westminster School of Art. During her five years in England she also enrolled in sketching classes in Cornwall and in Bushey just outside London. However in 1902 Emily's penchant for hard work aggravated her rapidly failing health and the last fifteen months of her stay in England were spent at the East Anglia Sanitorium in Suffolk.

Once studies in England were over Emily Carr was anxious to return to British Columbia. Back at home she was offered a position as a cartoonist for *The Week*, a weekly newspaper in Victoria, to which she contributed political cartoons and an occasional verse until she was offered a teaching post with the 'Ladies Art Club' in Vancouver in 1906. Although the teaching post was short-lived, Vancouver was to become Emily's home for the next four years. She successfully resumed her teaching of children's art classes and continued as time permitted in her own artistic endeavours.

In 1907, on vacation from teaching, Emily cruised to Alaska with her favourite sister Alice, stopping at several native villages on the way. The Indians and their art made 'Strong Talk' and her interest in both became more intense. It was on this trip that Emily Carr committed herself to documenting the culture of the Indians of British Columbia. She returned determined to preserve on paper and on canvas the Indian villages and their vanishing totems and she vowed to travel throughout the province to experience them firsthand.

Anxious to know about the 'New Art' which seemed to be taking France by storm, Emily closed her Vancouver studio in 1910 and in July of that year left for Paris, where she enrolled in the Académie Colarossi. The Post-Impressionist and

Fauve Schools were exactly the 'new way of seeing' that Emily Carr was looking for. With the guidance and instruction of Phelan Gibb in particular, and the 'moderns' in general, her brushwork, palette and attitude underwent radical change. The breakaway from the restraints of the more traditional art schools was exhilarating and for the first time she felt real progress was being made. Having returned to Vancouver she exhibited her latest French works in the spring of 1912 while re-establishing herself as an art teacher. That summer, intent on finding new material and anxious to apply what she had learned in France to her much-loved Indian themes, Emily embarked on her most ambitious and productive trip, a visit to the remote Skeena River region and the Queen Charlotte Islands. In these Indian villages Emily Carr gathered a wealth of images and impressions which would be a recurring focus of varying intensity throughout her long and prolific career.

At this time British Columbians were generally unprepared for any deviation from the English landscape tradition. Disheartened by what she considered to be a lack of acceptance of her new work in Vancouver, Emily decided to close her studio. She conceived the idea of building an apartment house in Victoria which would assure financial independence yet enable her to pursue her artistic endeavours more fully. Unfortunately the dream was short-lived. Hill House (later known as 'The House of all Sorts') was located on her father's property and was completed in 1913. It proved to be the bane of Emily's existence from the outset. The three apartments she let to the public were a never-ending source of irritation and consternation to her and she found little time to devote to her beloved painting in the studio she had incorporated into the design of the house. Both the First World War and the attendant slump in the real estate market contributed to a hand-to-mouth existence and for fifteen long years Emily struggled to make ends meet.

Frustrated at her attempts to remain financially solvent during this period, Emily resorted to a variety of activities in order to supplement her income. These included raising hens, rabbits, and well over three hundred English bob-tail sheep-dogs; growing vegetables, hooking rugs, and at one point running a ladies' boarding-house, which to Emily represented the ultimate indignity. It was also during these difficult years that she turned her attention to pottery, which she fired in her home-made kiln and sold through several tourist shops in Canada.

With the worst of this bleak financial period behind her Carr struck out on sketching trips again in 1920 to the West Coast of Vancouver Island and to points relatively close to Victoria. The landscape of home was becoming the predominant theme of her paintings at this time. Working in isolation Carr was still experimenting with the landscape techniques learned a decade earlier in France.

The turning-point in Emily Carr's career came in 1927 with the invitation to exhibit at the National Gallery in Ottawa in the Exhibition of Canadian West Coast Indian Art. Her trip to Eastern Canada to attend the exhibit brought her in contact with many dynamic people concerned with art in Canada. It introduced her to members of the Group of Seven and particularly Lawren Harris whose art had a profound effect on her.

The emotional support of Harris and the enthusiasm he and other members of the Group of Seven had for her work was a great boost to Carr. Inspired by the Group of Seven, Emily Carr returned to Victoria and took up her quest of the Indian culture with increased confidence and determination. At the age of fifty-six she embarked on the most prolific period of her career. That summer of 1928 Emily returned to Alert Bay, the Skeena River region and the Queen Charlotte Islands where, despite hardships and adverse conditions, she pursued her subject with a passion and returned home with a wealth of new sketches. A year later, on the suggestion of both Lawren Harris and Mark Tobey,

Emily abandoned her Indian themes, casting her eye toward the forests which seemed to hold a particular mystery for her.

From 1927 Emily began keeping a journal in earnest in an effort to clarify her thoughts. Writing, at this point, was for the most part an aid to her painting in that a certain idea, theme or event could first be illustrated in words and then reworked in paint. As well as drawing and painting, Emily had been writing in various forms since childhood. Doggerel verse or rhyming couplets were commonly found with her caricatures; often a word portrait accompanied a painted portrait. Her journals and sketchbooks were peppered with amateur verse, more often than not poking fun at herself. Her teachers, friends, family and pets were usually commemorated in this way.

Short-story writing began in the early 1920's. Always a very good storyteller, Emily began seriously to commit her experiences to paper with her enrollment in a short-story correspondence course with the Palmer Institute of Authorship in California in 1926. Her writing was helped by the constructive criticism of her three 'literary friends', Flora Burns, Ruth Humphrey and Margaret Clay.

By 1930 Emily Carr's two exceptional talents of painting and writing were running a parallel course. Her field trips yielded sketches which would later become finished oil paintings, and journals and notes which would later become published stories.

The sketching trips of 1929-1932 were confined to Vancouver Island. A variety of landscape themes captured Carr's attention in and around Victoria. A short walk from home was the sublime Beacon Hill Park. Further afield, studies were made on the west coast of Vancouver Island at Nootka and, on a separate trip, to the north-east coast of the Island. Both the Goldstream Flats and the Metchosin Woods inspired an outpouring of tree studies in 1931 and 1932. A profitable sketching trip was made to Cordova Bay in 1931

as well. From 1930 to 1933 Emily was most often accompanied on these sketching trips by her friend and only sketching partner, Edythe Hembroff-Schleicher. These years saw the execution of a number of sea and sky studies, predominantly oil on paper, an innovative technique which Carr had developed during her sketching trips of 1932. A journey to the Brackendale-Lilloet area in the summer of 1933 presented her with the challenge of painting the majestic mountains of British Columbia. Recognition of her painting was constantly increasing. Showings of her work were included in major exhibitions in London, Paris, Washington, and Amsterdam as well as in many centres in Canada.

Later in 1933 Emily Carr purchased an old caravan fondly called the 'Elephant'. This self-contained accommodation, which she had outfitted to suit herself and her pets, enabled her to spend several weeks in a location of her choice, sketching during the day and writing in the evening. With the 'Elephant' Carr devoted more time to the forest, trying to capture the feelings evoked by nature and the trees in particular. A growing spirituality augmented the pervasive technical strength of her work at this time.

From this point an explosion of creativity took her beyond the forest studies, past isolated elements to a full expression of her spiritual bond with nature. Now the underlying elements and energy, whether in forest, sea, or sky, were compressed and released.

As well as her painting, Carr's writing was undergoing significant developmental changes in the thirties. In an attempt to refine her writing style, Emily enrolled in a short-story-writing course at Victoria College in 1934. Her lifestyle also shifted dramatically when twenty-two years of 'landladying' were brought to a close in 1935 with the sale of Hill House. Financially, physically and emotionally, the sale of the 'House of all Sorts' was a relief.

With the severe blow of her first heart attack in January 1937, Emily found her painting activities curtailed. This was countered to some degree by the tremendous success of her exhibits, particularly her first solo exhibition at the Vancouver Art Gallery in 1938. The strain of preparing for numerous exhibitions resulted in a stroke the following year, which hospitalized her for two months. Recovering from this attack, she once again set out for her favourite sketching spots in the woods and countryside of lower Vancouver Island. However her output was only a fraction of her pre-heart-attack field-trips.

In this year Emily moved to her sister Alice's house. Built on the original Carr property just a stone's throw from her birthplace, this house was to be Emily Carr's final residence. The upheaval of the move precipitated another heart attack and the strain of her sketching trip to the nearby countryside later in the year resulted in a major stroke.

Although often confined to bed in the years 1937 to 1945 Emily Carr courageously directed her energy to writing. With the interest and encouragement of her friends, she produced an astonishing number of short stories in this period. She became increasingly serious about her writing and began sending short manuscripts to various publishers.

In 1940 a selection of Emily Carr's Indian stories were read on CBC radio, first by Dr. Sedgwick, Head of the English Department at UBC, and then by his assistant, Ira Dilworth. It was with the careful editing and guidance of Ira Dilworth that this eminent painter's first book, *Klee Wyck*, was published in 1941.

This series of short stories focusing on her trips to various Indian villages in British Columbia between 1898 and 1928 had been written over a period of eleven years. As with her painting, her writing described British Columbia and particularly the Indians in a new and original way. Emily's affinity for the Indian people, her wit and keen perception contributed to the wide appeal and enduring success of *Klee Wyck*, which in 1942 won the Governor-General's award for non-fiction.

With the publication of *Klee Wyck* Emily Carr became known not only as a gifted and unique artist but also as a talented writer capable of touching the lives of people the world over.

Following a two-year absence from the woods and buoyed by the success of *Klee Wyck*, Emily felt well enough to resume sketching. Two highly compressed and creative periods were spent in Mount Douglas Park in the spring and summer of 1942. Here she was inspired by the coastal landscape and especially the monumental cedars of this forest; but again this took a major toll on her health. Confined to bed she persisted with her writing. Later that year her second book was published, a collection of short stories primarily about her childhood in nineteenth-century Victoria, entitled *The Book of Small*. A juxtaposition of staid Victorian society and the freedom and beauty of nature is a constant pattern in this as in all her books. Especially apparent in *The Book of Small* is Emily's passionate interest in animals and nature which developed early in childhood and remained with her throughout her life. Her thoughts and descriptions are precisely conveyed through original images in a captivating prose style that is simple, clear and direct. As with her painting at this time, her writing was carefully pruned of all but the essential elements. *The Book of Small*, like *Klee Wyck* before it, was an instant success.

From the wealth of manuscript material which Emily Carr had been revising for years a third book, *The House of All Sorts*, was published in 1944. All the warmth, pain and pathos of 'landladying' and raising sheep-dogs is brought to light, touched in retrospect by the author's lively sense of humour.

Emily Carr died on 2 March 1945, just months after the publication of *The House of All Sorts*. At her request her autobiography, *Growing Pains*, which had been written over the course of several years between 1939 and 1944, was to be published posthumously. Written in the inimitable style of her previous works,

Growing Pains was received with enthusiasm by a devoted public. Other posthumous publications followed with *Pause: A Sketch Book* and *The Heart of a Peacock*, both appearing in 1953. Transcriptions from Emily Carr's journals composed between 1927 and 1941 were combined to form *Hundreds and Thousands*, released in 1966. Written as a diary, the entries are very personal and specific. What emerge are the day-to-day joys, challenges, and disappointments which faced Emily Carr, her searching and striving for understanding and expression of the world around her. A religious, contemplative, questioning artist is revealed.

Her death in 1945, at the age of seventy-three, marked the passing of a courageous, vibrant woman whose talents live on in her art and in her writing. At the time of her death, Emily Carr was generally recognized as Canada's foremost woman painter and writer; today her stature as one of Canada's greatest artists remains undiminished, the power of her vision remains undimmed.

Victoria, 1984   KERRY MASON DODD

1 *Ucluelet Inlet, Vancouver Island*

The first village I ever visited many years ago was that of Ucluelet on the west coast of Vancouver Island. It was at seven o'clock
on a cold misty morning in early spring. I was just a young girl
invited to visit at the Mission House for some sketching. A very
big man in a very little canoe took me from the steamer to the
house, a lonesome little dwelling with its face to the sea and its
back to the dense forest abounding in panthers.

EMILY CARR'S NOTEBOOK, 1913

2 *Kispiox, in the Skeena district*

3 *Kispiox, in the Skeena district*

You must be absolutely honest and true in the depicting of a totem for meaning is attached to every line. You must be most particular about detail and proportion... Every pole in my collection has been studied from its own actual reality, in its own original setting, and I have, as you might term it, been personally acquainted with every pole....

EMILY CARR'S NOTEBOOK, 1913

4 Skidegate, Queen Charlotte Islands

5 *Skidegate Inlet, Queen Charlotte Islands*

The Skidegate Inlet is lovely—in places it is quite narrow and also very shallow needing a very careful stearsman. . . . We were followed up almost the entire inlet by large shoals of porpoises who gambolled round the boat with mad antics and made a splendid sight, leaping as they did right out of the water.

EMILY CARR'S NOTEBOOK, 1913

6 Kitseguecla, in the Skeena district

They liked me to paint their poles and were interested and friendly. In very few instances have I met with surly behaviour. Though twice I have been met with a very threatening attitude and told to leave the village. They accused me of stealing their poles but with a little tact and jollying on my part and even at times a present of a duplicate sketch, we have always become the best of friends.

EMILY CARR'S NOTEBOOK, 1913

7 *Kitwanga, in the Skeena district*

I glory in our wonderful west, to leave behind me some of the
relics of its primitive greatness. These things should be to we
Canadians what the ancient Briton's relics are to the English.
Only a few more years and they will be gone forever into silent
nothingness and I would gather my collection together before
they are forever past.

EMILY CARR'S NOTEBOOK, APRIL 1913

8 *Skidegate, Queen Charlotte Islands*

9 *The village of Haida, Queen Charlotte Islands*

There is a great dignity about the Haida people. They take life more seriously than most tribes. It was interesting to note that the faces of their totems were more austere and grim in appearance. I only saw one smile.

EMILY CARR'S NOTES, NO DATE

10 Kispiox, in the Skeena district

These poles are fast becoming extinct. Every year sees some of their number fall, rotted with age; others bought and carried off to museums in various parts of the world. Others alas, burned down for firewood. In some instances the Indians are becoming ashamed of them fearing that the white people whom they are anxious to resemble will laugh at them . . . .

EMILY CARR'S NOTEBOOK, 1913

11 Kispiox, in the Skeena district

12 *Kispiox, in the Skeena district*

13 *Kwakiutl house posts from Kingcome Inlet, now in Stanley Park, Vancouver*

Where did the Indian find that great Art of his? Not in academics, or travel, or pictures, or books. He got it from profound observation, absorption of his material by all of his five senses. Only when he had made himself familiar with his material from bones to skin did he venture to express the thing in his art.

EMILY CARR'S NOTES, NO DATE

14 *Chief Skedan's mortuary pole from Skidegate,*
now in Stanley Park, Vancouver

Old legends were depicted on some of the totem poles, a legend
that had always been connected with that particular family.
These are very, very hard to learn; many of the younger Indians
do not know them: others again are unwilling to tell. It is indeed
always an honor and a privilege to be taken into an Indian's confidence for they are, and have good reason for being, suspicious of
the whites.

EMILY CARR'S NOTEBOOK, 1913

15 Kitwanga, in the Skeena district

My heart was *so* happy up in that country. My old trip into
Skeena did so much to bring things clear and fresh. Those calm
quiet eagles *so strong*. Did you notice the turn of their heads—
such a twist of power.

EMILY CARR TO IRA DILWORTH, 1943

16 Kitwancool, in the Skeena district

The dead are buried in the ground and perfect little miniature houses are built over them, having chimneys, windows, doors, etc. Within you will see all the treasures of the dead: clothes, sewing machines, children's toys, women's hair, warrior's weapons, dishes, boots, hats.... This cemetery is divided into little streets. The little houses of the dead are gaily painted; no two are alike in colour and design. They also have little gardens round them.

EMILY CARR'S NOTEBOOK, 1913

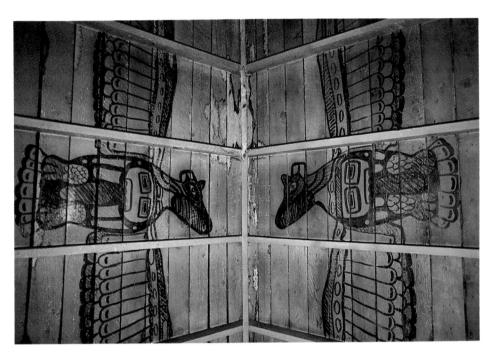

17 *'House of All Sorts', Simcoe Street, Victoria*

On the whitewashed underside of the roof shingles of my attic
room I painted two immense totemic Indian Eagles. Their out-
stretched wings covered the entire ceiling. They were brave
birds, powerful of beak and talon. Their plumage was indicated
in the Indian way; a few carefully studied feathers painted on
wing, breast and tail gave the impression that the bird was fully
plumed. Sleeping beneath these two strong birds, the stout west-
ern maple tree beneath my window, is it wonder that I should
have strong dreams that folded me very close.

EMILY CARR'S NOTES, NO DATE

18 Rainforest, Vancouver Island

Oh, I wanted to paint in those woods. They whirled and swirled and skimmed and went into deep places and mystery.

EMILY CARR TO IRA DILWORTH, AUGUST 1944

Sketching in the big woods is wonderful. You go in, find a space wide enough to sit in and clear enough so that undergrowth is not drowning you, then, being elderly, you spread your campstool and sit and look around. 'Don't see much just here—wait!' Out comes a cigarette—the mosquitoes back away from the smoke. Everything is green—everything is waiting and still. Slowly things begin to move, to slip into their places. Groups, masses and lines tie themselves together; colors you had not noticed come out timidly or boldly.

EMILY CARR'S NOTES, NO DATE

Though everything was so still, you were aware of tremendous forces of growth pounding through the clearing, aware of sap gushing in every leaf, of push, push, push, the bursting of buds; the creeping of vines. Everything expanding every minute, but doing it so subtly you did not actually see anything happen.

EMILY CARR'S NOTES, NO DATE

What hearst thou?
Whisperings, murmurings, now
loud, now soft, the trees talking,
squeakings, groanings, creakings
sometimes tree trunks chafing
against each other, the saucy
screech of blue jay, the kingfisher's
clatter and the chatter of an
occasional squirrel, resenting my
intrusion.

FOUND IN EMILY CARR'S 1936 JOURNAL, DATED 14 AUGUST 1929

What do these forests make you feel? Their weight and density,
their crowded orderliness. There is scarcely room for another tree
and yet there is space around each. They are profoundly solemn
yet uplifting joyous. You can find everything in them that you
look for, showing how absolutely full of truth, how full of reality
the juice and essence of life are in them. They teem with life,
growth, expansion. . . .

EMILY CARR'S JOURNAL, 1934

19 *Rainforest, Vancouver Island*

20 Cathedral Grove, Vancouver Island

The world stands there like a patient child while the rain pours, drenches, washes, soaks rotten things back into earth to start all over again.

EMILY CARR'S NOTEBOOK, 1913

Here is a picture, a complete thought—and there another—and there. There is everywhere something sublime, something ridiculous or joyous or calm or mysterious. Tender youngness laughing at gnarled oldness, moss and ferns and leaves and twigs, light and air, depth and colour—chatting, dancing a mad joy dance, only apparently tied up in stillness and silence.

EMILY CARR'S NOTES, NO DATE

21 *Rainforest, Vancouver Island*

22 *Canneries, Skeena River*

The canneries are in sheltered coves. Even the new ones look old.
The West Coast weathers them soon. We twist and turn among
the Islands. The sun plays hide and seek. The shacks here and
there are grey and forsaken and broken; thrown together quickly;
as quickly disintegrated. Fragile and temporary in contrast to the
solidity and enduring of the sombre forests.

EMILY CARR'S JOURNAL, 1929

23 *Opitsat on Meares Island, south of Nootka, Vancouver Island*

Nootka like all coast cannery towns straggled atop the water's edge; behind the town was dense forest well timbered and heavily undergrowthed. There was only one path through the forest. It ran to I don't know where. Behind that path there were only deer trails. I went into the forest to paint. It was desperately lonesome and silent until suddenly a man came crashing through the undergrowth. He halted almost on top of me as tremendously astonished to see me as I to see him. In broken English he shouted, 'One lady, she paint, this wood?' . . . the creature did not know I was as indigenous to these woods as a pine tree.

EMILY CARR'S NOTES, NO DATE

24 *Quatsino Sound, Vancouver Island*

We lived on fish and fresh air. We sat on things not meant for
sitting on, ate out of vessels not meant to hold food, slept on
hardness that bruised us; but the lovely wild vastness did something to us all. I loved every bit of it—no boundaries, no beginning, no end, one continual shove of growing—edge of land
meeting edge of water, with just a ribbon of sand between. Sometimes the ribbon was smooth, sometimes fussed with foam.
Trouble was only on the edges; both sea and forest in their depths
were calm and still.

EMILY CARR'S NOTES, NO DATE

25 *Port Hardy, Vancouver Island*

The boat was anchored out a way and we landed one at a time in the small dug out canoe. I made a quick summary of the work to be done and was already deep in a sketch by the time the others were landed. Here I may say that this is one of the trying features of this work. You must therefore come quickly to your conclusions, select your objects . . . time is so precious you dare not stop to rest up nor think how tired you are. In places where there is much walking you must shoulder a very heavy pack. The elements always have to be buffeted; wind, showers, hot sun, incoming tides.

EMILY CARR'S NOTEBOOK, 1913

26 Mount Finlayson, Victoria

I do not think that most artists could tell what was their aim in art exactly. It just grew and grew from a small beginning. This is especially true in a great country with much unbroken newness to explore. It necessitates much digging and searching, burrowing as deep as one is able and the using of our hearts as well as our eyes.

EMILY CARR'S NOTES, NO DATE

27 *Cathedral Grove, Vancouver Island*

Tree boles pillared the forest's roof, and streaked the unfathom-
able. Forest like, gigantic rain streaks pouring; the surge of
growth from the forest's floor boiled up to meet it. I peered at it
through the uncurtained window while the Missionaries prayed.

EMILY CARR'S NOTES, NO DATE

28 *Rainforest, Vancouver Island*

29 Cathedral Grove, Vancouver Island

Organized turmoil of growth; that's what those thick under-growth woods are and yet there is room for all. Every seed has sprung up and put itself into its own space, poked itself up through the rich soil and felt its way into the openest space within its reach, no crowding; sharing its space, part of the scheme. . . . There is nothing to compare with the push of life.

EMILY CARR'S JOURNAL, 16 JANUARY 1936

30 Cathedral Grove, Vancouver Island

31 Goldstream Park, Vancouver Island

The wood was dark and sombre but somehow a stray sunbeam had filtered through. The effect in that dark wood was both beautiful and weird.

EMILY CARR'S NOTEBOOK, 1913

32 Cathedral Grove, Vancouver Island

Grey days in the mossy wood are very fine. A rich yellow gold carpet of moss and these straight purplish tree stems with dull green tops—very lovely.

EMILY CARR'S 1940–41 JOURNAL

Long vistas of scraggy leavings and fallen trees . . . mountains
here and mountains there; close ones fir covered and green, far
ones cloud topped and blue as the Heaven that meets them. What
a lot these quiet stretches of logged off left-to-itself land had to say.

EMILY CARR'S JOURNAL, 1940–41

33 Near Port Renfrew, Vancouver Island

34 Cathedral Grove, Vancouver Island

When the light broke through the cedars it was like a key unlocking delight.

EMILY CARR'S JOURNAL, 1940–41

The roof was high and as blue as eternity itself. The green walls trembled with life. Whisperings ran round the galleries. The standing pillars were holy with mystery. The organ was loudest when the wind blew.

EMILY CARR'S JOURNAL, 1939

Those solemn woods sloped down and down and down towards the sea. I got some fine big tree work there, immense boles rearing into the divineness of far above tops. Lying directly under Heaven itself you knew the blue sky pressed down upon the green black top branches that those powerful boles beheld. The solid masonry of these heavy, cathedral-like woods with their sensitive ghost plants mysteriously pushing through the pine needle mould.

EMILY CARR'S JOURNAL, 1940–41

There was a wide happy peace in John's field and behind was great stretches of second growth land, fuzzy young firs with brilliant new yellow green tips on every bough all upward curves and circles. An occasional old veteran with a battered droop to it, grim and stark, throwing its arms against the sky. Spindly poles of trees with little tufts on top but no lower boughs. Trees that had been too blemished or insignificant for the loggers to bother with swaying in the wind as if they wanted to tickle the sky.

EMILY CARR'S JOURNAL, 1940–41

35 *Second growth, Little Qualicum Falls, Vancouver Island*

36 Stanley Park, Vancouver

But, there's always something new to see in the woods and glory in. I hope sincerely I shall be able to go to them again bye and bye. I like fresh goods not canned.

EMILY CARR TO EDYTHE HEMBROFF-SCHLEICHER, 13 MARCH 1937

37 *Stanley Park, Vancouver*

38 Mount Douglas, Victoria

Woods you are very sly picking those moments when we are
quiet and off guard to reveal yourself to us, folding us into your
calm. Accepting us to the sway, the rhythm of your spaces, space
interwoven with the calm that rests forever in you. For all that,
you stand so firmly rooted, so still . . . .

EMILY CARR'S NOTES, NO DATE

A big idea was rising in me out of the dawn of nowhere. When-
ever I had any spare time and on Sundays I used to go into Stanley
Park which was very big, very wild, and very beautiful. It was the
places far off from people and houses that appealed to me and I
took Billie and went.

EMILY CARR'S JOURNAL, 1940–41

Canada is a land of spacey sweeps of thousand mile spreads of fir trees, wild mountains, tearing rivers: a land of terrific silences.

EMILY CARR'S NOTES, NO DATE

39 Sproat Lake, Vancouver Island

40 Sooke, Vancouver Island

There is room to breathe; space to feel out into and think.

EMILY CARR'S JOURNAL, 1929

41 Sproat Lake, Vancouver Island

All the grand trees have gone, just the stumps with their row of
jagged screamers. . . . The little trees are bobbing up everywhere,
young and fluffy, merry and proud—the gawks and the misfits
who were too poor for the forest murderers. Still misshapen
heads patronize the little trees as the great trees patronized them
long ago.

EMILY CARR'S JOURNAL, SEPTEMBER 1934

42 *Cordova Bay, Victoria*

43 *Stanley Park, Vancouver*

44 Beacon Hill Park, Victoria

The autumn woods are like people of sixty when great pleasure comes to them and ease after struggle. They plump out with mature richness and have a last fling at wearing gay colours before they drift into 'don't care.'

EMILY CARR'S JOURNAL, AUGUST 1935

I expect the woods about you are pretty now all the leaves are tumbling. I used to love to kick them to rustling and pretend I was a lady in silk petticoats.

EMILY CARR TO EDYTHE HEMBROFF-SCHLEICHER, 16 OCTOBER 1935

45 Witty's Lagoon, Vancouver Island

Off we started towing the old van behind us. We halted at some definite spot I had previously selected. It was never very far from Victoria, no more than ten or twelve miles. Off the highway my requisites were isolation yet within walking distance of some means of transportation, running water, safety and freedom for the creatures and woods and sky for my work. I think these were the very happiest days of my life. The quiet and freedom, the opportunity of concentrating on my work, the living in the very heart of what I loved.

EMILY CARR'S JOURNAL, 1940–41

46 *Witty's Lagoon, Vancouver Island*

Next spring I moved the van...a clear stream in a little wood, wide daisy patches, sweet briar rose bushes, sheep nibbling, the sound of the sea and a great stretch of sandy beach; perfect setting.

EMILY CARR'S JOURNAL, 1940–41

47 Howe Sound, north of Vancouver

I was going to Bucaneer Bay to stay with a friend and on the way
I stayed overnight at the Indian village of Sechelt. I had with me
my old bobtail sheepdog and a great white cockatoo, Sally, who
loved trips and travelled in a basket portmanteau. Sometimes
Sally chewed a hole and popped out her crested head and
exclaimed, 'Sally's a Sally', which embarrassed me very much.
I hated being laughed at by the public.

EMILY CARR'S NOTES, NO DATE

48 *Goldstream Flats, Vancouver Island*

Goldstream Flats lay between hills. The sun came in late and
passed out early. The flats were lush with green. A river ran
twisting though broadening out through marshland as it
approached the Saanich Inlet. A rough little river rattling noisily
over boulders bursting over and under fall logs, hurrying over
broad pebbledly places, having as many moods as turns. A long
winding path up the valley was peopled by magnificent trees;
maple, cottonwood, pines and spruce, all of a great age and heavily mossed.

EMILY CARR'S JOURNAL, 1940–41

49 Goldstream Park, Vancouver Island

In the clearing where the tall slender pines with blobs of greenery
on the top shoot up from among the stumps of great great grand-
fathers I watch the slender boles. They sway from the root with a
circling movement in the sky, stirring the clouds round and
round with their bunched tops—very peculiar. They make a loud
swishing sound.

EMILY CARR'S JOURNAL, 1940–41

This place is full of cedars. Their colors are terribly sensitive to change of time and light. Sometimes they are bluish cold green then they turn yellow warm green. Sometimes their boughs flop heavy and sometimes float—then they are fairy as ferns and then down they droop, heavy as heartaches. No wonder Emily despairs.

EMILY CARR TO IRA DILWORTH, AUGUST 1942

50 *Goldstream Park, Vancouver Island*

51 Goldstream Park, Vancouver Island

Over us the skies were high. From the Point you saw across the sea the Cascade Mountains. I spent part of May and the month of June out in the van and did a lot of open sky studies. At night when the turkeys and the sheep had gone home to their farm and the dell below me lay black and silent except for the secrets whispered between the sea and the trees I would sit among the sleeping creatures in the van, my feet on a biscuit tin that contained a hot brick, the little lamp above me, and write.

EMILY CARR'S JOURNAL, 1940–41

52 *Esquimalt Lagoon, Vancouver Island*

53 *Metchosin, Vancouver Island*

We are becalmed among the cows. No matter how the wind or rain batter, the calm of the cow persists; endless chewing, swing, coil, flop of tails.

EMILY CARR'S 1938 JOURNAL, 12 JULY 1938

The cows are another joy. I am sure I have far more in common with them than with the ordinary lady. . . .

EMILY CARR TO NAN CHENEY, 25 JULY 1938

54 Prospect Lake Road, near Victoria

55 218 St Andrew's Street, Victoria

56 *Coast Mountain Range, north of Vancouver*

Spring is lovely this year. I have been out into the real woods twice—taken and left; no one within miles. The spring coloring is so fleeting—changes every day.

EMILY CARR TO IRA DILWORTH, MAY 1942

Spring does seem to be trying its best to make up for some other shortcomings in the world. Just now even my tiny garden is gay though my big maple umbrellas it entirely.

EMILY CARR TO IRA DILWORTH, APRIL 1941

57 Moresby Island, Queen Charlotte Islands

Oh it seems to me flowers were the exquisite finish off of all God's creations—a last bit of His own self thrown in for good measure. After the people, the beasts, and the birds, then the silent radiant harmless loveliness without flaw or naughtiness like the rest of us.

EMILY CARR TO IRA DILWORTH, JANUARY 1942

58 *Beacon Hill Park, Victoria*

My home was on the edge of Beacon Hill Park and I loved it like my own garden. A low rounded hill covered with broom, the world never looked such a round complete little place as from the top of Beacon Hill. Water could be seen east, west, south. Nearer mountains were purple; farther mountains, blue. On the north lay the city backed by Cedar Hill and Mount Tolmie.

EMILY CARR'S JOURNAL, 1940–41

59 Beacon Hill Park, Victoria

On Good Friday I walked Alice in the park and felt rather tired. We went to see the spring flowers. The Pollies are simply glorious by the stream and the Rhododendrons just bursting and all sorts of fancy fruit blossoms. I try to picture everything as vividly as I can to Alice as we go along having to be very careful not to annoy her by 'blind talking' . . . Poor souls what a great affliction blindness is.

EMILY CARR TO IRA DILWORTH, APRIL 1942

60 *Beacon Hill Park, Victoria*

61 Beacon Hill Park, Victoria

On the smaller of the two lakes lived a pair of Royal swans presented by King George V to Victoria. They did not mix with the mob of swans and ducks in the larger lake. Woo resented the airs of these aristocrats and protested furiously if I took a few crusts to them. Crowded on a low flat stone among the water lilly leaves, she watched the gliding approach of their majesties. As the great male swan flattened a hissing beak towards the crust floating on the water, Woo pounced and delivered a hefty crack across his majestic cheek, opening her mouth to its limit and staring into his eye. She then grabbed the crust while their majesties backed out among the lilly pads very embarrassed at having been smacked by a jungle beast.

EMILY CARR'S JOURNAL, 1940–41

62 *Beacon Hill Park, Victoria*

Spring was young; I over seventy. With spring all about me I sat
sketching in the clearing that was now given over to second
growth, baby pines, spruces, hemlock, cedar and creeping vines,
fireweed and bracken. . . . I could no longer scramble over great
logs nor break my way through networks of brambles, creep
under bushes and drown myself crown high in lush young
growth. I had to be taken out, sat down and called for which was
a nuisance but I got immense delight in just being there in the
quiet wood, nobody for company but Spring.

EMILY CARR'S NOTES, NO DATE

63 Dallas Road, Victoria

I had a great pleasure yesterday, but one that exhausted me and for which I pay today. Mrs. Royal took me in my chair to the beach off Dallas Road. I got out of the chair and sat on the steps with the beach spread below. The air was glorious. I did not expect to see that beach ever again. It is one I loved.

EMILY CAR TO IRA DILWORTH, JULY 1944

64 The Olympic Mountains from Dallas Road, Victoria

It is not the objects portrayed that make a picture. Group them in ever so successfully. Design the forms and colors. They please the aesthetic sense, the beauty sense, satisfy the eye. That is not enough. They must say something to the soul to justify their existence as a picture, set up a yearning and a longing for something; an ensemble that has been suggested and holds one either consciously or subconsciously.

EMILY CARR'S JOURNAL, 10 DECEMBER 1935

65 *Arbutus, Dallas Road, Victoria*

Grand, red trunked arbutus, very old and gnarled, tying themselves into an agony of knots and nobs. With the shining smooth-
ness of their satiny young leaves bunchingly springing in fanlike
arches, absorbing a glint and sparkle of sun and sky into themselves, holding it in the polished surface of each leaf, dandling
the reflected blue as the leaves swayed back and forth till the
trees were as much blue as green and the red of the bark was
redder for having burst and showing the delicate green yellow
new skin underneath. The Arbutus were so upspringing and gay
standing among the rocks or in open exulting, spreading their
branches to the sky, inviting and reflecting the sky.

EMILY CARR'S JOURNAL, 1940–41

66 *The Carr House, 207 Government Street, Victoria*

At six years of age my world was a really splendid place. Seven acres of fields and woods and a garden and a great yard full of creatures. The spotted cow with twin calves, Peter the pig who munched acorns so delightedly, rabbits and chickens and dogs and cats and the trees with the birds nests in them.

EMILY CARR'S NOTES, NO DATE

I had a lovely out in my chair yesterday . . . all round the hill. We went right up into a part behind where the peacock pen is. They were squealy and lovely. Then we went through nice woody trails, quite wild, broom and bracken and dirt paths. I live it over and over. It was so delicious. I did not think I'd ever go again.

EMILY CARR TO IRA DILWORTH, 25 MAY 1944

67 Broom, Vancouver Island

Oh life, I feel so like a beaten up old drift log driven too high ashore by a mighty wave for any wave to reach it again.

EMILY CARR TO IRA DILWORTH, 1943

68 *Witty's Lagoon, Vancouver*

69 Driftwood, Long Beach, Vancouver Island

Hipi's rude shack of drift had for foundation forest giants who, shorn and mutilated yet rebelling, tore themselves groaning from the booms going north and were tossed high above the tide by a great storm.

STORIES: WRITING SCHOOL LESSONS, 1927

70 Metchosin, Vancouver Island

Go out into your own lovely woods and look up. Forget the mud of the earth and remember the space and glory of the sky.

EMILY CARR TO IRA DILWORTH, 15 DECEMBER 1944

71 *Lake Cowichan, Vancouver Island*

72 *Emily Carr's grave, Ross Bay Cemetery, Victoria*

To have been permitted to give pleasure by writing and painting the plain simple things of my life fills me with the deepest gratitude; that these things spoke so that I might hear and in a language I understood even a little of.

EMILY CARR TO IRA DILWORTH, 14 FEBRUARY 1942

73 *Cordova Bay, Vancouver Island*

74 *Sunset from Mount Douglas*